GARDEN OF THE HEART

*A Spiritual Journey
in Poetry*

Lux Interpreti Publishing
20280 N 59th Ave., Suite 115
Glendale, AZ 85308
www.luxinterpreti.com

Photography: Getti Images

Cataloging-in-Publication Data is on file at the Library of Congress.

Olson, Dora

Garden of the Heart:

p. cm.

ISBN 978-0-9888471-1-8

ISBN: 978-0-9888471-1-8

First Printing February 2014

Printed in USA

Distribution by Lightning Source

DEDICATION

This collection of poetry is dedicated to my children and grandchildren. May they each find their own Garden of the Heart, that centered place that waits to embrace them with Unconditional Love.

GARDEN OF THE HEART

*A Spiritual Journey
In Poetry*

By
Dora Olson

Lux Interpreti
Publishing

CONTENTS

GARDEN OF THE HEART

A Spiritual Journey

in Poetry

DEVOTIONAL
POETRY

THE GARDEN

Love lit a candle in my desolate Heart
and created a sanctuary for Thee.
Love pulled the weeds of negligence
for a small garden of refuge for me.

Love opened a window for heavenly Light
to dispel any shadows or lies,
and that inner space and my garden place
both lit up under heavenly skies.

Love lit a fire for warmth to melt
cold memories of yesteryears,
which flooded my Heart with gratefulness
and watered my garden with tears.

This Love now calls me each morning
to come to the garden and pray.
And when I do, I pray to You,
please, Lord, let me stay.

LIGHT AND LOVE

Thank you for the Garden
of my Heart where I can go
and wait for You to light
the spark of Love within my soul.

The Light is not just seeing,
it's the mind that becomes clear.
The Love is not just feeling,
it's the melting of all fear.

So thank you for the Garden
of my Heart where I can go,
where Light and Love both intertwine,
my Love is Yours, Your Light is mine.

THE DIFFERENCE IN ME

I turn from the lower and rise.
I rise toward the higher and see.
I see the Light from the middle
and smile at the difference in me.

The highest is far from my knowing,
but it beckons me higher you see.
It calls me to rise to the middle
and smiles at the difference in me.

DEVOTION

There is no beguiling mystery
coming from my pen,
just devotion from my Heart,
pure and simple, now and then.

THE RIVER

I am not a poet, a writer, an artisan of words,
but a singer of sonnets that long to be heard,
that wait to be picked like flowers that grow
on the path to my Heart where the river flows.

A river of Life that flows through my veins,
a river of Truth no book can contain,
a river of Light no mind can sustain
is this river of Love that no one can name.

SIMPLICITY OF LIFE

What do I have in my Heart today
that I would be willing to give away?
My Heart is so full with abundance galore,
I'll just give it away and trust You for more.

There is plenty of space for me to embrace
all the things in life I don't want to face.
I can't change the world, but I can change my mind,
to turn from pride and just be kind.

I can turn from greed and plant a seed
that gives its fruit to those who need.
I can turn from desire to gratefulness
and give the world my happiness.

I can turn from fear, from doubt, from worry
and find my mind is in less of a hurry.
There is plenty of time, so I'll give mine.
The simplicity of life is simply divine.

What do I have in my Heart today
that I would be willing to give away?
My Heart is so full with abundance galore,
I'll just give it away and trust You for more.

YOUR WILL

I imagine Your will to be a river of Love,
endlessly giving until it overflows in us,
and we must also give ourselves away to life
until there is nothing left but oneness with You.

YOUR WORLD

When I turn to You, Lord, and can get out of my own way, I experience a clarity of mind like a different world opening to me. I call this Your World because it's not about me.

In Your World, I let go of my pride and arrogance, suddenly thankful that I don't have to know everything, that I don't have to fix everything, that I don't have to destroy evil,

For You are the Creator, You are the Sustainer, and You are the Destroyer of everything but Love.

In Your World, I let go of my greed and striving, full of contentment and surprise at how easy it is to give when I'm not comparing and measuring my own share,

For You create the abundance in the world and You hear the needy. I have been tasked to simply let go.

In Your World, I have no desire for things to be different, just a deep knowing that Your will, and not mine, is the perfect answer to every prayer,

For You have led me to this path and shown me such grace that I no longer want anything else.

In Your World, the chains of the past are broken, the fear of the future is forgotten, and I am free, for the fear turned to trust in Your Unconditional Love.

Your World is subtle, but it is not elusive. It seems to be hidden but waits to be found when I turn to You, Lord, and remember to get out of the way.

MY HEART DECIDED TO STAY

Turned to You I rise
but turned away I fall.
I'm finally starting to get it
and now I'll give it my all.

Wherever I move my attention,
it seems that's where I go.
Whatever I focus my mind on
is what I come to know.

You are the force that pulled me
when I turned my mind Your way.
You are the Love that filled me
when my Heart decided to stay.

THE ME JUST SLIPS AWAY

Dark is my fear for the future
and regrets related to past.
Fear is my own dark prayer to God
to somehow make me last.

But Light is my trusting spirit.
It's all about You, Lord, not me.
Like night from day, You light the way
to finally set me free.

For when I turn from fear to Love,
from ignorance to Truth,
my past regrets, my future fears
all turn to dust and I can trust.

And in that trust, I learn to live
a different kind of way.
Loving You and all I see,
the me just slips away.

I SOMETIMES WONDER

I sometimes wonder if the highest part of me
is not the inner core, the most tender Heart,
covered by a shell thickly layered and hardened
by all the wounds of life.

Layer after layer of fear and ignorance,
one laid by a victim, one laid by a judge.
So many emotions hardened by suffering
that nothing could crack that shell but You, Lord.

Then the soft protected seed, watered by tears,
its hardened shell opened by Your Love,
begins a new life of compassion for all who suffer,
grateful for the protection of that flawed outer shell.

TAPESTRY OF LIFE

Thank you, Lord, for using -

Our weakness and Your Strength,
our darkness and Your Light,
our fear and Your Love,
to weave a beautiful tapestry of life,

Where dreams are woven into stories,
where flaws are woven into perfection,
where conflict is woven into peace,
and diversity is woven into One.

SET ME FREE

I have lived in material darkness
with only a spark of You for Light.
I have lived in a world of material dust
with only a thread to You for Life.

Each moment a gift of the senses
to see, to touch, to hear,
stretching the thread through another hour,
another day, another year.

Although I treasure these moments
as the gifts they were meant to be,
it's time to surrender the thoughts and cares
the world has given me.

Then I can leave with nothing
for time will set me free
from pride and greed, desire and fear
and every thought of me.

EYE OF THE NEEDLE

I am not afraid of death,
for I die to my self each day
as I turn from me to You,

Shedding my burdens of pride and passion,
giving You everything that I fear
and everything that I Love,

Readying myself for the day
when this broken shell
will fall away,

And at the eye of the needle,
You will pull me through,
thin as the thread attached to You.

LISTENING TO THE HEART

If it touches your Heart, let it fill you.
If it brings you to tears, let them flow.
Whether pleasure or pain, let it reach you,
let it teach you, then let it go.

If it touches your Heart, then live it.
If you love it, don't settle for less.
Turn away from the fear that distracts you
for the Heart offers only the best.

If it touches your Heart, then embrace it.
Let it flow through your being like a song.
Whether happy or sad, just listen,
and when you're ready, just follow along.

PRESENT MOMENT

I turn from the mind of time
to the Heart of Timelessness
and cling to the present moment with You,

A living oasis between
the dead past and unborn future
that You have made to share with all creation.

I IMAGINE

I imagine that You heard my child-like prayers
and in compassion taught my mind to see
that if it turned from thoughts of fear to Love,
it could soar to heights known only by the free.

I imagine that You smiled at my fidgeting mind,
but in the meditative silence You reveal
that to truly surrender even a moment of time
is the moment in which I begin to heal.

I imagine that You laughed at my various paths,
but in the middle I find You so near,
where Your Love shines out so brightly
that I can almost see Heaven from here.

All You wanted from my prayers was a thank you.
All You wanted from meditation was my time.
All You wanted from my path was that it turn
toward You so that all I'd ever see would be divine.

TRUEST FRIEND

I ask only to live a true and sincere life,
true to my Heart and sincere with You,
for You already know my weaknesses, my sorrows,
and remember my strengths when I cannot.

No need to hide or pretend with You, my friend,
for You know my lowest thoughts, my highest dreams.
Yet You stay with me always, always,
my truest friend in my Heart.

FREE TO ROAM

My mind's tendency is to be free to roam,
not chained to mindful thoughts.
But since I cannot keep it chained,
I will at least keep it aimed toward You.

GATHERING WOOL

My mother used to call it gathering wool,
sitting still and letting my mind wander,
remembering everyone I have ever loved
and putting them in my Heart.

I gather my family and friends,
my children, my grandchildren,
and put them in my Heart.

I gather each mother's child,
the innocence of humanity,
and put them in my Heart.

I gather the beauty and harmony of the world,
the wonder and mystery of the cosmos,
and put them in my Heart.

And when all is gathered, I give my Heart to You
and let all that I love merge into the great Love,
the boundless Love, the unconditional Love,
that lasts beyond the limits of time.

DESIRE

Perhaps my life
will never be without desire,
either material aspiration that begins in the mind
or spiritual inspiration that begins in the Heart.

But if I cannot be free from desire,
then free me from the mind's desires.
If I cannot know, then free me
from the pride of thinking I know.

If I cannot have, then free me
from the greed of needing to have.
If I cannot be more, then free me
from the fear of not being enough.

EVERYTHING FROM YOU

At long last I see that all is from You,
all a gift, all a grace, all for free.
You ask from me nothing and just keep on giving.
I'm a glass trying to hold in the sea.

My Heart is so full that it just overflows.
It makes me want to give too,
to write it, to sing it, to shout it on high,
but everything comes from You.

We are reflections, but You are the Light.
We are sparks, but You are the Flame.
We make the effort, but You make it right,
and our lives are not lived in vain.

FREEDOM TO BE

When I turn from me to You
and the me recedes from sight,
all that is left is freedom to be
an instrument of Your Light.

Suddenly I am an open Heart
in a centered place above,
where You show the truth of who I am,
an instrument of Your Love.

We are all the tools, the instruments
of Your will, whatever it be.
Some give themselves away to life
in humble harmony.

Many turn from cruel to kind,
some heal wounds with their forgiveness,
while others stay in school to learn
their path that leads to happiness.

When I turn from me to You
and the me recedes from sight,
all that is left is freedom to be
an instrument of Your Light.

IN SPITE OF ME

I will plant seeds of Love wherever I go
and never look back at what I sow.
For good comes from good no matter what I see,
and God will make it right in spite of me.

DUALITY

It seems in this world,
my Heart's desire to give
is always shadowed
by my mind's desire to receive.

FLY AWAY

It is said there are two kinds of thought:
constructive or destructive,
uplifting or degrading, high or low.

I don't want to know
how low my thoughts can go,
so I turn my thoughts to You and fly away.

PERHAPS A DREAM

I wonder if my soul still resides in the garden,
a paradise of selfless purity and grace, bliss and love,
only dreaming this life to experience the fall
into an opposing self, a nemesis of selfishness,
that seeks the knowledge of good and evil
and creates what lies on the other side of paradise.

Perhaps the me is a momentary illusion
because it is here and gone in a moment of time,
one heart-stopping, breath-taking,
or mind-awakening moment,
when the me I see is but a part of a world
visible only in a dream of duality.

THE OTHER SIDE

So much Love and Light here where I hide
from my pride and greed, desire and fear.
I have found a peaceful realm within,
so near, right here, on the other side of me.

I am humble here and kind, content and giving.
I am grateful here, accepting, trusting and forgiving.
It's a paradise, a kingdom, a heaven in my Heart,
so near, right here, on the other side of me.

HOPING

I turn within for Peace to flow through
this material self that surrenders to You,
kneeling in the Garden, waiting at the door,
hoping for the Joy to come once more.

I turn within for Truth to shine through
this shadowed mind that searches for You,
listening in the Garden, waiting at the door,
hoping for the Light to shine once more.

I turn within for Love to flow through
this humble Soul at one with You,
singing in the Garden, waiting at the door,
hoping for the Heart to open once more.

THE MYSTERY OF YOU

Let my mind turn to You
and finally come to see
that the mystery of You, Lord,
is more interesting than me.

Let the Oneness of Your Spirit
hold my mind's attention
as it intertwines with all the world,
fulfilling Life's intention.

Let my mind surrender
to the things it cannot know.
Let it bow to the Heart
when Love begins to flow.

Let my mind grow up, Lord,
from the straying adolescent,
from the prodigal son or daughter,
and return to the Present.

Let my mind turn to You
and finally come to see
that the mystery of You, Lord,
is more interesting than me.

A CANDLE

In the stillness,
You light a candle in my mind.

But when I turn from its Light to write,
the winds of thought blow it out.

FREE TO IMAGINE

Turning from fear to Love
sets me free to imagine again as a child,
to question without needing to know,
to explore without fear of being lost.

For only the Heart can inspire the mind
to contemplate something higher than the self
and turn the winds of thought
from me, to we, to One.

CONTEMPLATING ME

THE IMPERFECT ME

Thank you for loving the imperfect me,
this little primate evolved from the sea,
growing a mind that is striving to be
more than this little imperfect me.

I want to be more than a crazy ape
with an animal mind that loves to hate.
So I contemplate and postulate,
with no one here to translate.

But You heard me, Spirit, and taught from afar,
a world within near the Morning Star.
You taught me to take my hand from the jar,
to trade my small view for visions afar.

You taught this monkey mind to still,
to practice patience and wait until
the day would come of strength and skill
to turn from self and choose Your will.

So thank you for loving the imperfect me,
this little primate evolved from the sea,
growing a mind that's beginning to see
that I am more than just the imperfect me.

DEEP, DEEP DOWN

In my youth, I sought acceptance
for I was afraid I was unacceptable.
I hadn't learned to think for myself,
so I followed a friend or a trend.

But deep, deep down,
I knew the acceptance I sought
would not be found
unless I found it in my heart.

In my middle years, I sought purpose
for I was afraid I had no purpose.
I was ambitious and proud
and greedy for success.

But deep, deep down,
I knew the purpose I sought
would not be found
unless I found it in my heart.

In my older years, I sought truth
for I was afraid I had lived a lie.
I sought truth in books,
in beliefs, in traditions.

But deep, deep down,
I knew the truth I sought
would not be found
unless I found it in my heart.

I have lost many battles to fear,
but You have since dried all my tears.
For all that I sought was finally found
deep, deep down in my Heart.

THE SUFFERING ME

My life has been a journey of return
to another world, a realm of Love,
where a Mother or Father waits
for the child to come home from school.

And perhaps I will be asked
what it took a lifetime to learn,
that my ignorance of Love
created the suffering me.

That the suffering me, feeling alone,
created pride and desire to comfort itself.
But pride created intolerance
and desire created unhappiness.

That the suffering me, feeling lack,
created greed and fear to protect itself.
But greed created poverty
and fear created violence.

Until the suffering me cried to realize
that it had created all the suffering in the world.
And in that unselfish thought I awakened
for Compassion had opened my Heart.

FELLOWSHIP OF THE HEART

I wish that I could find a place
where all who love God could pray
together with others of every faith,
setting worldly beliefs aside for the day.

They could stand or kneel or prostrate low,
but all would rise to share
their overflowing love for God
and joy would fill the air.

Whether they speak or sit in silence
or join in song and dance,
there would be no mistrust or division.
There would be no pride or arrogance.

For all would join in worship
with open hearts and open minds,
holding hands to take a stand
for the unity of mankind.

I wish that I could find a place
where all who love God could pray,
where His Love would bring us together
in His unconditional way.

THE CALL TO LOVE

There is One that calls us to Love
with all our hearts, with all our souls,
with all our minds, and with all our strength,
for Love is deeper than words, higher than beliefs.

Some let their hearts pray in the garden with Jesus
for the healing of Love.

Some let their souls sing and dance with Krishna
in the joy of Love.

Some let their minds listen at the feet of Buddha
to the wisdom of Love.

Some let their strength practice Abraham's
obedience to Love.

These were all called in the name of Love.
I will not turn against them in the name of religion.
My war is against my own dark tendencies,
and I surrender only to the One that calls us to Love.

SYMBOLISM

Would we fall from the grace of God if we turned
from the symbols that we place on Him in our minds,
symbols that would bind Him exclusively to ourselves,
to one name, one culture, one people?

Perhaps it is we who are bound
to a savage quest for eternal life,
freed only by the Love
that lives eternally in the Heart

If God is indeed everywhere,
then He must live in every Heart
shining the Light of Divinity
in every man.

Perhaps in turning from the symbols in the mind
to the reality in the Heart we can see this Light
and be unable to herd others into box cars,
hack them with machetes, or atomize them with bombs.

LET ME TURN

Let me turn away, veer clear away
from fear and its virulent infection of hate
that would fill me with odious and unmelodious
ramblings and rumblings
to shame my written words,
profane my spoken words,
and desecrate even the silent words
of my thoughts.

I DARE

Dare I think that I could live from the Heart
in a world being pulled apart by fear?
Dare I think that I could wield a sword of words
to pierce the veil of darkness in this world?

First I must balance on its razor's edge
turning from my lower self to pledge
a fight for freedom, freedom to live, freedom or die,
for I am ready to fight for freedom from my own self,

To fight my own pride, check my own greed
that spread intolerance and disparity in the world,
to turn from desires and childish fears
that create enemies and violence in the world.

Dare I think that I could live from the Heart
in a world being pulled apart by fear,
without first surrendering to Your sword of Light
to pierce the veil of darkness in my own mind?

I CHOOSE LOVE

Knowledge does not necessarily
lead to wisdom or truth,
but Love does both
so I choose Love as my path.

Wealth does not necessarily
create happiness or still desires,
but Love does both
so I choose Love as my treasure.

Law does not necessarily
create justice or stop injustice,
but Love does both
so I choose Love as my duty.

Religion does not necessarily
allow compassion or follow conscience,
but Love does both
so I choose Love as my religion.

AWAKENED

I am awakened when the me,
this material extension of my spiritual self,
turns within to its Source,

When its machine-like heart surrenders
to a Heart of Love,
when its computer-like mind opens
to a Mind of Compassion,
when its material self bows
to a selfless Soul.

I am awakened when the me,
this material extension of my spiritual self,
turns a one-pointed mind toward You,

Perhaps to see a glimpse
of the Higher Mind's Understanding,
perhaps to hear a whisper
of the Soul's Truth and Wisdom,
perhaps to feel a touch
of the Heart's Love and Oneness with You.

WHO AM I?

Who am I but a needy little me,
awareness tethered to a body,
aware of only me.

Who am I but an arrogant little I,
awareness entangled in a mind,
aware of only thoughts.

Who am I but a freedom seeker,
wanting to turn to the Heart and come undone
as I become aware of only You.

Who am I but a fledgling spirit ready to fly
above the physical world, above the mental world,
into the spaciousness of the Heart.

LITTLE CORNER OFFICE

I have a little drama queen, my E-G-O.
She troubled me a lot, tried to run the show,
until I gave her the title of C-E-O
of that little corner office in my mind.

She still puffs out with opinions and pride,
but not like before when something inside
would explode with self-righteous indignation
and out she'd come for a confrontation.

She still peeks out with a greedy eye,
watching for gain is her modus operandi.
But when I ask for a count of the blessings of life,
she goes back to the office and counts all night.

She still sneaks out with burning desire,
trying to set my mind on fire.
Get up, get going, get out there and be.
I just sit back and smile. I'm finally free.

She cries now and then with doubt and fear.
What's going to happen without me here?
I say get up, get going, get back to the grind.
I need you in the office, that little corner office
in my mind.

CONTEMPLATING WE

LIGHT AND GRACE

Turning from me, I awaken to see
a whole new world on this path to Thee,
where I feel only humbleness in being a part,
no pride in self that keeps us apart.

I feel so content as I watch this world share
that gone is my need to measure and compare.
I feel so grateful to be embraced by You
that desires to be different are released as untrue.

I feel no fear as I turn from me,
just forgiveness and trust in the world of we,
this awe-filled present mind and place
that is opened and turned to Your Light and Grace.

LOVE FOR LIFE

Where I live, there is a beautiful tree
that gives itself away to me,
a vision of beauty, hosting birdsongs for pleasure,
growing fruit for my body, giving shade for my leisure.

Under the outstretched arms of that magnificent tree,
I felt it giving its gifts to me.
Then I sensed its willingness to also share truth,
so I watched and listened under its silent roof.

Each life is a gift to be given away,
not stored for self, for it will just decay.
You must give your gifts in the time that you live
for that is when you have gifts to give.

Life gives its self as a sacrifice,
no fear of death, just love for life.
There is no fear in the world of we
under the outstretched arms of that magnificent tree.

THE WORLD OF WE

The veil of fear in the mind of man
divides two very different lands.
One is dark in fear for me,
the other Light in awe of Thee.

I ride the dark on the wings of thought
of yesterday or tomorrow,
filled with fear and always fraught
with worry and pending sorrow.

I am weary of traveling the speed of mind
and turn to the speed of Light,
where my mind turns inside out to see
a subtle shift to the world of we,

Where I see and hear Your harmony,
I smell Your earth, I taste Your sea.
I'm alive and in Love with all I see
in this awesome world of we.

With just one turn, my mind is free
as the world of we embraces me.
I could feel sweet Love for eternity
when I turn from self for a glimpse of Thee.

GARDEN OF LIFE

I live in a desert environment
where the land is scorched by Mother Nature
and scarred by human nature.

But if I am still and quiet, I can see
extraordinary creatures living ordinary lives
right in my own back yard.

Just a blink of an eye startles the quail
into the air or into the brush
where tiny chicks are herded and rushed.

A young road runner can forget to run
and fly awkwardly into a tree,
then turn and coo like a dove at me.

I have watched bees cut circles out of leaves
and roll them into little barrels
that they can hardly lift without a breeze.

A coyote thins the rabbits, there's a falcon in the sky,
and a rare javelina raids gardens nearby,
plus snakes and scorpions and lizards, oh my.

Lord, they are beautiful, wild and free,
yet they know to share the water
and wait for the rain together.

Let me walk softly on this earth as they do,
leaving no mark of pride, no scar from greed,
in this Garden of Life we call home.

TO BE

The butterfly has its day to play,
emerging from a cocoon of darkness
as a transformed ethereal being
that lifts its tenuous wings and flies away.

The flower has its day to play,
blooming in pompous and carefree splendor,
flaunting its beauty, its color, its fragrance
before it bows to the world and blows away.

Each spark of life has its day to play,
to create a moment of celestial beauty
in a stark and barren world
before it tips its hat and fades away.

To play it again? Could be,
since life has such an affinity to be.
Oh, I would love to be a butterfly.
No, a flower. No, a tree.

SING IN THE CHOIR

Let me listen and hear the song of my Heart
and turn from the mind of desire.
Not to know more, have more, or be more,
I just want to sing in the choir.

CHILDREN OF GOD

I contemplate the idea of two little children,
one says "me first," the other says "You first,"
and Love embraces them both.

The outer child is one with the Mother,
attached to the senses that fill its world,
a material child that returns to the earth.

The inner child is one with the Father,
attached to the Love that fills its Heart,
a spiritual child that returns to the Light.

The material and spiritual children of God,
twin vines twisted together into a tree of life,
growing from the earth and reaching for the stars.

CHILD IN MY HEART

Children are like diamonds in the rough,
not yet shaped by the world, nor polished by beliefs,
but shining on the inside so brightly,
they reflect Your Light through their eyes.

I think there is a child in my Heart
calling my mind to turn,
to come inside and play and delight
in the hide-and-seek beauty and oneness of life.

My body is nearly dried fruit,
but sugarplums still dance in my head
when I turn to the child in my Heart instead,
and Your Light shines again in my eyes.

STILL FREE

I walk the line of the divided mind
to see both sides of me,
the me conditioned to the outer world
and my inner self, still free.

Each morning I turn to the hinterland
where Love was born and I began,
an inner place where I'm free to explore
within and beyond these material shores.

I catch glimpses of beauty, snippets of rhyme,
the words at sunrise can touch the sublime.
But somehow words don't sound the same
in a mind conditioned to a world in chains.

Soon it cuts and pastes and even erases
my truth, my love, and finally replaces
my words with just its arrogant views
and I fail to recall the words of my muse.

So I walk the line of the divided mind
to accept both sides of me,
the me conditioned to the outer world
and my inner self, still free.

FROM ME TO WE TO ONE

Let me turn from me,
for its not about me.
I am but a part of we
and we are one with You.

Let me turn to You,
within to perceive You in my Heart
or out to perceive You in the world,
for there is no place that You are not.

Let me turn from the divided mind of me
to the present mind of we
to the one-pointed mind toward You,
from me to we to One.

CONTEMPLATING

ONE

LOST IN THOUGHT

My mind gets lost in a thousand words,
dividing the oneness and labeling the diversity.
So I turn from words to experience
the simplicity and oneness of life.

I turn from a word called me,
for me is just part of the wholeness of we.
And wholeness is undivided oneness,
and One is the word for You.

My mind gets lost in a thousand meanings
until it turns within to find true meaning
in a wordless experience that captures
the simplicity and oneness of life.

FREE FROM ME

When the divided mind turns from me,
who is thinking so clear, who is feeling so free?
Is it me? Is it I? Is it all an illusion?
Just wanting to know is causing confusion.

When I turn to You and face Your Light,
the shadow of self disappears from sight.
There is nothing to block or cloud Your reflection.
Only me thinking divides the perfection.

Turning from self, all thoughts are gone,
only peace is felt in the Light of Your dawn
of a new day with no shadows, where all is free,
awareness of oneness, with no thoughts of me.

IN THE CENTER

My mind wonders on You,
if You are the order in the chaos,
the oneness in diversity;
if You are the abundance in the emptiness.

It wonders if You are life arising from death,
if You are the Light in the shadows.
My thoughts go on and on until my mind
finally wonders if You are everything.

If You are both the order and the chaos
and You protect us in the center.
If You are both the abundance and the emptiness
and you provide for us in the center.

If You are both the shadow and the Light,
before the beginning and after the end,
creating and renewing over and over,
and sharing it all with us, in our center.

TIME

Mind is the time and place of diversity,
billions of lives experienced differently,
but the Heart is the place of oneness
where the One embraces us all.

In time we begin, expand, and diminish
but timeless oneness is where we finish,
when mind is free to accept and embrace
the reflection of God in every face.

Mind is the time and place of diversity,
billions of lives experienced differently,
but the Heart is the place of oneness
where the One embraces us all.

LOVE'S SWEET EMBRACE

Who poured the fluid darkness of my mind
into the fiery circle of my Heart,
creating this swirling dance of opposites
like muddy water and holy oil that cannot mix?

Be still mind and come to rest
in the warmth of the ambient Light.
Come and wait for Love's sweet embrace
to dispel the lies and shadows that you fear.

And when yin and yang, dark and light,
and all apparent opposites disappear,
I will leave a teardrop of my sorrow in the light
and a teardrop of my joy in the darkness,

To remind me of this sacred time and place
where Heart and mind find balance face to face,
and all our dueling differences are erased
by Love's sweet embrace.

EVER-EXPANDING CIRCLE

I choose the ever-expanding circle of the Heart,
no longer to follow the serpentine mind,
winding and spiraling in the universe of time,
doing the math, doing the math,
creating and destroying everything in its path.

I choose the ever-expanding circle of the Heart,
no longer willing to add or subtract
into images or words, symbolic abstract
that will never eclipse the shining circumference
of the ever-expanding circle of the Heart.

DANCING IN THE LIGHT

I imagine the Heart as an Ocean of Love
meant to fill a vast and empty mind.
An inland sea is this mind of me
bound within this small material entity.

I imagine this sea as a mind divided,
one part filled, one not yet filled,
one part joyful consciousness dancing in the Light
and one unconscious shadow crying in the night.

OUT OF TIME

Every valley of death in fear I must cross,
every mountain of perfection I must climb,
will all be embraced by the Heart someday
when the mind has run out of time.

There is a lake of fire in the mind of desire,
but it will all be surrendered to the sublime,
to the cool clear waters of the Heart someday
when the mind has run out of time.

SPIRITUAL PHYSICS

Turned to the outer world of body and mind,
I am a momentary expression of the divine,
a particle blipping in and out of time.

Turned to the inner world of Heart and Soul,
I am a timeless reflection from above,
a wave in the Ocean of Your Love.

ONE POWER

I sometimes wonder if the One Power flows
through Heart and Soul and stretches the Mind
into the farthest reaches of the universe of time.

Perhaps it fills the Heart with the spirit of *Love,*
anoints the Soul with the spirit of *Wisdom,*
and guides the Mind with the spirit of *Understanding*.

Perhaps it centers in stillness for *Purpose of Counsel*
before manifesting into life as *Power and Knowledge*,
then dividing in diversity as the spirit of *Fear or Awe*.

I experience the fear and separateness in the mind,
but turn back to the Heart and the oneness of Love,
the Light of Awe, for the clarity of knowing,

That life is not about a separate me,
but about the One Power that flows through life
in and through everything I see.

CLEAR PATH

Each day I wake in the divided mind of me,
free to choose fear or awe,
to dream or awaken.

So I turn within where Your Light shines
through Heart and Soul and Mind
to light the way back to You.

FIRST AND LAST

I contemplate the Spirit of Love
born first to last until the end of time,

An unwavering Light that shines
deep in the Heart of all creation

With the burning desire of the first One born
to shepherd the last one home

SEEDS OF LOVE

These words are seeds of Love.
They were born in the fire of my Heart.
They came on the wind to my Mind,
and they will grow wherever You decide.

ACKNOWLEDGMENTS

I would like to thank my son, Charles, whose love for wildlife led me to find a healing stillness in nature.

I would like to thank my son, Jesse, whose love for art led me to express my own love through words.

I would like to thank my son, Lucas, whose love for music led me to listen to the songs in my heart.

And I would like to thank my daughter, Rebecca, whose love for children gave me my greatest joy, three little grandchildren.